INTRODUCTION

FEW PROPERTIES *can claim to have been as central to the life and work of their owners as Down House. Charles Darwin and his family lived here in comparative seclusion for forty years during which time he wrote the majority of his major works including the most famous,* On the Origin of Species.

Why did Darwin settle on Down House as the base for his life's work? He spent five years of his life as a young man on his voyage around the world aboard the Beagle, *from which he returned famous, and then another five living in the social whirl and professional intensity of London. By 1842, also married by now and with two children, he knew he needed a retreat.*

The home he hankered after would be in the countryside where he could follow his particular method of working: examining and re-examining the minutiae of the natural world day after day. He was a countryman at heart, and loved to see the changing seasons, to breathe clean air, keep a few cows and create a garden. He also needed a place where he could shun all society if he chose and tailor the pace of his life to the unrelenting symptoms of his illness.

Down did not appeal immediately to Darwin or his wife Emma on an aesthetic level, but they had the financial means to adapt it to suit their needs and Darwin knew instinctively that, with some alterations, this could form the perfect home. In a letter written soon after moving to Down, Darwin wrote:

> *'My life goes on like clockwork and I am fixed on the spot where I shall end it.'*

One of the most striking features of Darwin's life here was the way in which he combined an unusually close involvement with his family of eight children with his prodigious scientific achievements. Even Darwin's study was not sacrosanct: the children were allowed to run in and out for items they needed. Rather than being hindered in his work by the children, Darwin seems to have drawn constant pleasure, comfort and inspiration from them and even used detailed observations of them in his books.

Wandering from room to room of the house, and through the grounds, the visitor gradually acquires a sense of the mind and personality of Darwin the scientist, but also of Darwin the husband and father. The two can never quite be separated. So many of Darwin's letters, diaries and possessions are displayed in the historic rooms and the exhibition here, that the experience of being inside his former home is quite a vivid and direct one.

This book tells the story of Darwin's life at Down House, showing how it became an integral part of his life and work. The opening pages give a tour of the historic downstairs rooms and the grounds, guiding the visitor through Darwin's study and billiard room, the drawing room and dining room as well as the gardens, orchards and Sandwalk. The second part of the book tells the story of Darwin's life, putting the house in context. It also includes plans of the rooms and a family tree to orientate the visitor both geographically and historically.

HISTORY OF THE HOUSE

FOLLOWING CHARLES DARWIN'S DEATH IN April 1882, the members of his family who had been living there moved to Cambridge, but Emma continued to spend most of each summer at Down until she died in 1896. After this the family kept the house until the turn of the century though they seldom went there. It was then leased to various tenants, most notably Olive Willis who founded the Downe House School for Girls in 1907. Her success and ultimate departure for larger premises in 1922 brought concern for the future of the house. Darwin's eldest two sons, William and George, had died during the previous decade and his remaining children were elderly. Another school mistress set up a school at Down, attempting to capitalise on Miss Willis's achievements, but Miss Willis had taken the prestigious name 'Downe House School' with her when she left, and her successor could not match her reputation. Downe House School still flourishes today under its original name.

When the house had been empty for some time it came to the attention of the Master of Darwin's old college, Christ's, Cambridge. He wrote to Sir Arthur Keith, then Conservator of the Hunterian Museum at The Royal College of Surgeons of England, saying that he thought the 'house ought to be a national possession', and asking whether Keith knew 'of any means by which this can be brought about?' Sir Arthur made a plea on behalf of Down during his presidential address to the 1927 meeting of the British Association for the Advancement of Science (BAAS). He did not have high expectations of success, but the result was a

telegram from George Buckston Browne indicating his willingness to provide the necessary funds to preserve Down House as a National Memorial.

Later knighted for his contributions to surgery, Buckston Browne took on the responsibility for the first renovation of Down House. He removed all the extraneous structures erected during its time as a school, and systematically set about establishing the house as a memorial to Darwin. He paid the purchase price of £4,250, also contributing some £10,000 for repairs and another £2,000 to serve as an endowment for the estate. Buckston Browne entrusted Down House to the care of the BAAS who opened it to the public on 7 June 1929. Dr. O J R Howarth, Secretary to the BAAS, was the first resident [Honorary] Curator and Sam Robinson was the first Custodian. Dr. Howarth and his wife Eleanor lived in the spacious first and second floor apartment, and Sam Robinson, with his wife and children, lived first in the staff cottage and then, from 1939 until his death in 1958, in the custodian's apartment in the old servants' wing. Sydney Robinson, Sam's son, maintained the house and kept it open for visitors until his retirement in 1974. Dr. Howarth and his wife compiled a scholarly account of the parish of Downe (1933) and remained here until his death in 1954.

Down House was reopened after the War. Sadly, Sir George Buckston Browne had died at the age of 94 in 1945 before the opening. Without his energy, commitment and resources, it was not long before the British Association was looking for an alternative stewardship. Expenditure exceeded income and the endowment fund, reduced in value, seemed sufficient to cover only existing debts, not urgent repairs. Various options were considered and the only organisation willing to take on the

project at the time was the Royal College of Surgeons of England. The College felt obliged to accept responsibility for the property as Sir George Buckston Browne had built a Surgical Research Station on land adjoining the College and presented it to them.

Down House was maintained by the Royal College of Surgeons for forty years. During this time Sir Hedley Atkins, former President of the Royal College of Surgeons, and his wife, did much to bring the property back to life. Sir Hedley was obliged to undertake major roof repairs and substantial redecoration, as both had been badly neglected since Buckston Browne's attentions thirty or forty years before. Lady Atkins had a particular interest in the garden, which flourished under her care. Following Sydney Robinson's retirement, Philip Titheradge became Custodian and, with Sir Hedley, kept Down House accessible to an ever increasing visiting public. Like Dr. Howarth, Sir Hedley also published a scholarly book entitled *Down: Home of the Darwins* (1974). Like Dr. Howarth's booklet, it has long been out of print. In 1983 Sir Hedley, like his predecessor, ended his days in the place he had come to love.

In the late 1980s the College began negotiations with The Natural History Museum for a more permanent solution to the maintenance and management of Down House. It soon became apparent to the Museum that the house was in desperate need of significant repairs. The roof was again in need of attention and visitor facilities were sadly wanting. With academic enquiries increasing, and an interest in wider use of the property testing the limited resources, it was clearly time for action. The Trustees of The Natural History Museum concluded an arrangement with English Heritage, enabled through a substantial grant from The Heritage Lottery Fund. The project was finally realised through the crucial support of The Wellcome Trust who provided the essential funding to secure the property. Thus, in the spring of 1996 Down House was purchased by English Heritage.

English Heritage has undertaken a substantial programme of building restoration work and provision of visitor facilities. The ground floor rooms have been recreated to look as they would have done in Darwin's time and the restoration of the garden is still underway. The first floor, previously closed to visitors, houses an extensive exhibition about the life and work of Charles Darwin and the theory of evolution.

TOUR OF HISTORIC ROOMS

'Aunt Bessy in the Drawing Room at Down.' An illustration by Gwen Raverat, Darwin's granddaughter, from her book Period Piece *(1952)*

The Drawing Room at Down House

Introduction to the Tour

DOWN HOUSE AS WE FIND IT TODAY has been restored in a way which reflects the house as it was near the end of Darwin's life, showing the culmination of the alterations made by the Darwins over forty years of residence here (see pages 2–3).

The conservation programme carried out from 1996–8 has recreated the very special atmosphere of Darwin's home while providing greater access to the building.

In plan, the ground floor remains essentially as the Darwin family left it on Emma's death in 1896 (see back cover flap). The north wing was the last addition to the house, built in the autumn of 1876. Darwin asked his builder for 'a billiard room, with bed-room and drawing-room

above', joining the house by a long entrance hall, allowing the front door and porch to be moved to their current position. Visitors to Down House enter through this door and pass into the room now fitted as the ticket office and shop.

Later on, Darwin moved his study into this large room which then became known as 'The New Study' and this is where he worked for the last few years of his life.

As you leave the shop, turn right into the Drawing Room.

The Drawing Room

In September of 1857 the Darwins began to build a two-storey addition to the north-west facade. It was originally intended for a 'new dining room and large bedroom over it' because

they found that they had 'quite outgrown [their] old room'. It was completed by the following February and later in the year Darwin confided to Joseph Hooker, his close friend, 'My room (28 x 19) with divided room above, with all fixtures (and painted), not furniture, and plastered outside, cost about £500.' By the time the room was finished they had decided to use it for a new Drawing Room.

The initial decoration was rather plain: the freshly plastered walls were simply painted with distemper coloured with yellow ochre to allow for drying out before being papered. No trace remains of the original paper, but Darwin's correspondence gives some clues to his and Emma's tastes. In a rather amusing letter to their son William, Darwin wrote on 7 July 1859:

'Mama went up yesterday and brought down two such patterns, of the exact colour of mud streaked with rancid oil, that we have all exclaimed against them, and we have settled on a crimson flock-paper with golden stars, though unseen by me.'

The current scheme reflects the period after the north wing was added (1876) when the house was largely redecorated.

The furniture and furnishings are mainly items which were used by Darwin in this room and which were kindly given to Down House by members of the family when the house was first opened to the public in 1929.

'A GRAND PIANOFORTE'

The focal point of the room is Emma Darwin's grand piano. This is the second Broadwood piano she owned, arriving shortly after the room was finished in February 1858. Emma was an accomplished pianist and would play most days for her own and the family's pleasure. Her daughter Henrietta recalled that she 'had a crisp and fine touch... there was always vigour and spirit, but not passion'. Emma had once taken a few lessons from Chopin, probably during an extended family tour to Europe when she was a young woman.

The piano has been carefully conserved and replaced in the Drawing Room in approximately the same position it occupied when it first arrived over 140 years ago.

The Darwins were also fond of good pictures and determined to finish the room with 'some nice water colour drawings'. These were bought with the proceeds of the sale of one of two Wedgwood copies of the famous Barberini or 'Portland' Vase which were owned by them (there were about twelve copies in all). At either end of the wall behind the piano are portraits of Charles and Emma painted by George Richmond just after their marriage.

Turn right out of the Drawing Room into the Inner Hallway.

Emma Darwin's piano in the Drawing Room

The Inner Hallway

The present hallway was built in 1876. On the left-hand wall as you turn into the inner hall are several framed prints of Old Master paintings given to Emma after her sister died in 1862.

At the far end of the hall, near the garden door, is a cupboard which one of the children described in later life as, 'The place of all others where the essence of the whole house was concentrated'. Here were kept tennis racquets, parasols and croquet mallets. This also was where Darwin deposited old manuscripts that he did not want to throw away, including a preliminary sketch of *On the Origin of Species*. The children sometimes used the paper to draw on.

On the opposite side of the Inner Hall is the Study doorway. Turn left into the Study.

The cupboard under the stairs in the inner hallway where Darwin deposited his old manuscripts

The Old Study

Perhaps the feature that most attracted Darwin to Down House was the 'capital study'. It was to provide a sanctuary for his work for most of the rest of his life.

The room faces north-east and is sheltered from direct sunlight except for a few shafts which may penetrate the windows in the early morning. Darwin always worked here from around 8 o'clock until half past nine when he would retire to the Drawing Room to listen to Emma reading the family letters or passages from a current novel.

The decor and arrangement of furniture in the room has been preserved from 1929 when the ground floor of the house was first opened to the public after restoration by Sir George Buckston Browne. This initial restoration was achieved with the help of Darwin's son Leonard using a photograph he had taken during his father's lifetime. The furniture is nearly all original and was presented to the museum by various members of the family.

Darwin's habit was to work sitting in the high-back arm chair which he had raised up on an iron frame fitted with wheels. Here he wrote *On the Origin of Species* and several of his other works. He would sit with his feet resting on a foot cushion and with a cloth-covered board across the two arms of the chair to serve as a writing surface. The chair is situated in the north corner of the room in front of one of the cupboards on which stands his multi-shelf files and small chest of drawers containing various papers, letters or books. Darwin fixed a small mirror to the outside of the building between the two windows so that if he looked up he could see any visitors approaching before they reached the front door.

The screened area in the left-hand corner of the room was Darwin's personal 'privy'. As he was frequently ill, this meant he did not have to leave the room for water, bowls and towels.

The Pembroke table in the centre of the room was his worktable and aside from the wooden spool for string, made by his son Horace, a changing array of items including letters, papers and specimens usually cluttered the surface. Various bottles of chemicals and curiosities, as well as material on which he was working, were kept on the revolving 'drum' table between the windows and the shelves nearby. Darwin could reach anything he needed either from his chair or a low seat in front of the right-hand window where he would set his microscope up on the shelf.

A portrait of the botanist Joseph Hooker hangs over the mantle as it did in Darwin's time as well as ones of the geologist Charles Lyell and Darwin's grandfather Josiah Wedgwood.

The main collection of books is a selection from Darwin's library and is on loan from The Botany School at Cambridge, by arrangement with the University Library.

On leaving the Study turn left. The next door on your left is the Billiard Room.

Some shelves in Darwin's study

A magnifying glass that belonged to Charles Darwin

The Billiard Room

This room used to be the dining room, but during the time Darwin was staying at Moor Park, taking advantage of the "water cure", he became very enthusiastic about the game of billiards. Early in May 1858 he wrote to his son William, at Cambridge University:

'I have been playing a good deal at Billiards, and have lately got up to my play and made some splendid strokes!'

During a second visit to Moor Park the following February, Darwin came to enjoy the game so much that he bought a billiard table for Down House. He played with his sons, William and George, and the butler, Parslow. The younger boys Frank, Leonard and Horace also enjoyed knocking the balls about. Darwin was working intensely at writing up his 'Species theory' for publication at this time and obviously found the diversion of billiards very therapeutic.

A bureau in the Billiard Room with the butler's tray set with drinks

In a letter to George, who was away at school, Darwin described the billiard table and remarked that it looked 'very very nice and smart … all the extra things, as marking boards, rests etc. etc seems very nice … The whole affair has only cost £53.18.0s'. Frank later recorded that his father used proceeds from the sale of some Wedgwood slate reliefs and his father's gold watch to buy the table.

A major rearrangement of the reception rooms meant that the billiard table could be installed in the former Dining Room. The caricatures now hung in this room catalogue the controversy caused by the publication of *On the Origin of Species* (see also pages 40 and 41).

Turn right out of the Billiard Room and enter the Dining Room almost immediately on your left.

The Dining Room

In 1858 a large new dining room was created in the room to which the bay had been added in 1843. Here the mahogany dining table could be extended to seat family and guests more comfortably. The original Georgian-style glazing was replaced by large window panes for a better view of the garden.

Darwin's Billiard Room

Lunchtime, always at about one o'clock, was the focal point of the day. The family and sometimes as many as a dozen guests would gather around the table. After lunch Darwin would rest on the sofa, either here or in the Drawing Room.

On the sideboard are a platter and two tureens from the Wedgwood 'waterlily' set ordered by Darwin's mother, Susannah, from her brother's factory.

To the right of the mantelpiece hangs a portrait of Charles's grandfather, Erasmus Darwin, in its original position.

As with the other rooms, the furniture and decor were not particularly fashionable and had to satisfy Charles and Emma's divergent tastes. However, the pictures were mutually approved and included important family portraits, several of which remain in the collection.

Furniture and family memorabilia have been either given or loaned by the Darwin family.

The Dining Room

The Old Kitchen

Beyond the green baize door along the passage, was the domain of the almost legendary Parslow, the Darwins' butler. He was engaged in 1839 when Charles and Emma married, and remained in their service until he retired in 1875. He was considered by Sir Joseph Hooker, a regular visitor to Down House, to be 'an integral part of the family'. Parslow ran the household from the Butler's Hall, which was enlarged when the servants' wing was rebuilt in 1845. Other staff included Comfort, a gardener who doubled as coachman, succeeded by Lettington who remained at Down House for twenty years and assisted with some of Darwin's experiments.

From 1865 the kitchen was under the command of Mrs Evans, who was unmarried but given the title 'Mrs' in recognition of her position in the household. She later married and became 'Mrs. Somebody quite different', according to Henrietta Darwin, who was obviously bemused by the event.

The account books follow the convention of referring to some staff by their surnames and others by their Christian names, but details are often lost under the entry marked simply 'wages'. Various housemaids not otherwise recorded by

name were accounted for in this way. The Scottish nurse, Brodie, who looked after the children, came to Down House in 1842 with the family. She stayed with them until the death of ten-year-old Annie Darwin in 1851 when she felt too grief-stricken to remain. She retired to Scotland, but occasionally returned on long visits. Later, governesses or tutors were engaged to provide the children's education before the boys were sent away to school.

At any one time there were as many as a dozen servants employed in the Darwins' service, nine in residence in rooms mainly on the top floor of the house.

A tureen from the Wedgwood 'waterlily' set

CAMBRIDGE UNIVERSITY LIBRARY DAR 225.191

The Down House staff

You can now go upstairs to the first floor to see the extensive exhibition about Darwin's life and work.

TOUR OF THE GROUNDS

Car park

Main Entrance

Toilets

① ② ③ ④ ⑤ ⑥ ⑦ ⑧

Mᵁᶜᴴ ᴼᶠ ᵀᴴᴱ ᶜᴼᴺᵀᴱᴺᵀ ᴼᶠ DARWIN'S MANY BOOKS WAS formulated and tested in the garden, meadows and woods of this small estate or in the surrounding coutryside. It was the setting of Down House that initially attracted Darwin and he immediately set about changing any aspects he did not feel comfortable with (see pages 28–31).

1. FRONT DRIVE

When Darwin purchased the house its main entrance was on the north-west side and the approach to it along a carriage drive approximately along the route of the present path from the car-park. One of his first improvements was to move the entrance to its present position on the east front. This included lowering the road outside, changing the access gateways and enclosing the area for privacy within high flint and brick walls. Modest arrangements were made for turning a horse or trap, but in general the entrance gave no display of wealth or importance. The entrance was private and enclosed with a plain grass lawn and trees and creepers clothing the house facade.

2. THE GARDEN

The garden was Emma's domain. Henrietta Darwin recalls:

'The early memories that come back to me seem now to be full of sunshine and happiness. I think of a sound we always associated with summer, the rattle of the fly-wheel of the well, drawing water for the garden; the lawn burnt brown, the garden a blaze of colour, the six oblong beds in front of the drawing room windows, phloxes, lilies and larkspur in the middle, and portulacas, gazanias and other low growing plants in front looking brighter than flowers ever do now; verbenas and the row of lime trees humming with bees, my father lying under them; children trotting about, with probably a kitten and a dog, and my mother dressed in lilac muslin ....'

To the south-west of the house lies a small area of lawn, ornamented with the formal flowerbeds described by Henrietta, and a sundial near the house by which Darwin is said to have set his clocks. The flat area of lawn was used to play croquet and then tennis; there was a swing under the yews for the children and a pile of sand for them to dig in. The lawn was then open to the meadow through a simple metal bar fence and enclosed on both sides by low mounding, trees and shrubberies. This arrangement gave both shelter from the wind and seclusion, while allowing for views across the meadows. In 1873 the lawn was linked to the house by the addition of a furnished verandah.

When Darwin moved in, in 1842, the lawns were already planted with specimen trees such as the magnificent sweet chestnut, the mulberry by the house and the yew and scots pine. These were augmented by Darwin with banks of evergreens and other shrubs and flowers to lend the garden a more "retired and sheltered character". He also created the mounds, involving the whole family in shaping the earth, and relaid the gravel paths.

A line of old lime trees and shrubbery sheltered the grounds to the north and a long gravel walk ran from the house to the kitchen garden decorated on either side with flowers and roses. A metal rose arch survives at the path junction near the west end and the path returned to the house on the other side of the shrubbery.

Horace Darwin's 'Worm Stone' that can be seen in the garden at Down House

The 'Worm Stone', a stone quorn used by Horace Darwin, with his father's encouragement, to measure the continuous undermining of soil by earthworms, can be found in front of a large yew bush under the Spanish chestnut on the north-west edge of the lawn. It is possible that this may not have been its original position.

3. WALLED LAWNS AND ORCHARDS

In 1845 land was purchased from a neighbour to extend the orchard area north-west of the house. This was walled in flint and brick as protection from cold winds and allowed for the planting of fruit trees and flower borders along the walls.

A further purchase of land was made in 1881 again to extend the orchard area, and the walls were re-aligned. It was then possible to construct a boiler house and what was to be called 'the laboratory' against the back wall of the glasshouses where, in his old age, Darwin hoped to carry out further experiments.

A hard tennis court, built for the family, can still be seen at the bottom of the orchard.

Darwin's greenhouses

4. THE KITCHEN GARDEN

This long narrow enclosure is walled on three sides but hedged to the south to receive maximum sunshine. Originally part of the neighbouring meadow, it soon became a productive kitchen garden providing vegetables and fruit for the family as well as an ideal location for Darwin's experiments and study of the cultivation and breeding of plants. As usual he combined domestic interests with scientific ones.

Over 40 years he grew and studied an immense range of plants, not only looking at variation in flowers through selective breeding but at the detailed growth of seeds, roots, tendrils and fruit.

In 1863 he built a hot-house for orchids and other prized plants supplied by Sir Joseph Hooker, the Director of Kew Gardens and a close family friend. Later, further greenhouses with new heating systems were added, some of which remain.

5. THE GREAT MEADOW

This fifteen-acre field was bought by Darwin together with the house and gardens. Early accounts show his prompt expenditure on improving the ground by removing flints from the soil. There was a main group of trees near the house comprising beeches and hawthorns and specimen trees scattered about including a walnut and a cherry tree. Hay from the field was harvested each summer, first by hand and then, from 1873, by hired machines. The family horses, cows and donkey would also have grazed here. In Darwin's time the field was full of tall grasses, wild-flowers, bees and skylarks. Unfortunately it is not now as rich in wildlife as it was, but with careful management it should recover. The meadow was often used by Darwin for observation of plants and creatures.

The southern enclosure of the Meadow has, since about 1930, been a cricket field with pavilion. The far, triangular, corner enclosure was then planted with North American species of which few now remain. It was known as 'Little Canada'.

The walled orchard at Down was ideal for fruit-growing

6. THE SANDWALK

A strip of land adjoining the Meadow with a wooded bank of scrub and oaks already forming its south-western boundary, was acquired by Darwin from his neighbour, Sir John Lubbock. Darwin then fenced and extended it by planting hazel, alder, lime, hornbeam, birch, privet and dogwood to form a small wood. Bluebells, anemones, cowslips, primroses and "wild ivy" were encouraged by Emma Darwin to ornament the ground. Along the dark side of the wood Darwin had holly planted, and on the other side a low thorn hedge over which the view into the valley and woodland beyond could be admired, as it can today. A path was formed around the perimeter with sand from a small pit in the wood. Around this path Darwin would take his daily constitutional walks, thinking and observing as he went, followed by his fox-terrier Polly.

At the far end of the Sandwalk, there was in Darwin's time a wooden hut or summerhouse where the nursemaid would knit, while the children played "Red Indians" among the trees.

7. GREAT PUCKLANDS MEADOW

This field on the west side of the Sandwalk was not part of Darwin's estate, but there was a wonderful view from the Sandwalk across it and down into the quiet valley below. Like the Great Meadow it is crossed by paths which were also used by Darwin in his rambles.

8. SERVICE YARDS AND ENCLOSURES

To the south of the house was a series of yards, outbuildings and paddocks, used for the horse and trap as well as the house cow, chickens and pigs that provided for the family table. Many of these structures remain. Here too was probably located the hexagonal pigeon house, built in 1855 to Darwin's instructions, where he bred and studied over 32 kinds of pigeon.

A FORMIDABLE HERITAGE

The Darwin family coat of arms

Silhouette of Charles Darwin's grandfather Erasmus, indulging in a game of chess with his son Erasmus c.1780

RIGHT *Engraving of Josiah Wedgwood by S W Reynolds after a painting by J Reynolds*

FAR RIGHT *Erasmus Darwin, a painting by Joseph Wright of Derby (1734–97)*

BELOW *Etruria – the famous Wedgwood factory in Staffordshire*

CHARLES ROBERT DARWIN, the fifth of six children, was born on 12 February 1809 into the much approved union between Dr Robert Waring Darwin and Susannah Wedgwood (see family tree on back fold-out). Charles's father Robert, often referred to as 'The Doctor', was widely respected as a physician, well-connected among the Shropshire gentry and the new industrialists.

Dr Darwin's marriage into the famous Wedgwood family was the result of his own father Erasmus's friendship with the potter Josiah Wedgwood.

They met frequently at the Lunar Society. This extraordinary dining club was composed of some of the foremost intellectuals of the day, many of whom were scientists and also members of the Royal Society. They called themselves "lunatics" because they met monthly at the time of the full moon so that they would have light to see them home. There were

physicians, chemists, a silversmith, engineers and a geologist, but their interests crossed the boundaries of their professions to include the arts and philosophical thought. The Society included notable members such as James Watt and Joseph Priestley. The intellectual energy of its members was one of the forces stimulating practical innovation and invention in the drive towards the Industrial Revolution in Britain.

Charles Darwin's grandfather, Erasmus Darwin, was a well-known physician with a great interest in natural philosophy and what today we would call technology. His knowledge of plant physiology and observations on artificial and natural propagation led to his major written works in which he described plant reproduction in romantic verse. The most popular of his books was *The Botanic Garden, a poem in two parts: The Loves of the Plants* (1789), and the *Economy of Vegetation* (1791).

Josiah Wedgwood and Erasmus Darwin were both involved in the anti-slavery movement.

LEFT *A family portrait of the Wedgwoods, painted by George Stubbs while visiting the family at Etruria Hall in 1780. The woman on horseback is Susannah (Charles's mother)*

The most fascinating aspect of Erasmus Darwin's work, in view of the later contributions of Charles Darwin, was that he proposed a natural explanation for the origin and development of life. In his book, *Zoonomia*, he attempted to classify illnesses and the actions of the body and considered several themes that were later developed by his grandson: the movement of climbing plants; cross-fertilisation in plants and adaptive and protective coloration and domestication in animals. In a later work, *Phytologia or The Philosopy of Agriculture and Gardening* (1800), he speculated on the mechanisms of inheritance, anticipating the discoveries of Gregor Mendel (1822–84). Erasmus Darwin's remark on sexual selection is one that could easily have been attributed to his grandson: 'the final cause of this contest among males seems to be, that the strongest and most active animal should propagate the species which should thus become improved'.

The result of the marriage of Robert Darwin with Susannah Wedgwood was that Charles Darwin was born into a wealthy, socially secure family with all the associated privileges. This was late-Georgian England, the time of Jane Austen, Coleridge and the painter George Stubbs. Darwin's parents were typical of the emerging entrepreneurial upper classes whose life revolved around books and letter-writing, and dinners and dances at the homes of similar families in the neighbourhood. Conversation on these occasions would have included lively discussions about music, literature, politics and the revolutionary ideas of the day.

The Darwins and Wedgwoods held each other in great esteem. Josiah Wedgwood presented his friend Erasmus Darwin with the first perfect copy of the famous Portland vase. Charles Darwin's mother, Susannah, ordered a Wedgwood dinner service with a botanical, 'water lily' theme for the Darwin home.

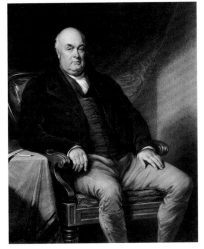

Robert Waring Darwin, Charles's father, in an engraving by T Lupton after a painting by J Pardon

The jasperware copy of the Wedgwood Portland Vase presented to Erasmus Darwin by Josiah Wedgwood

Childhood

THE PRIVILEGE AND SECURITY OF Charles Darwin's childhood, spent with his own large family at The Mount in Shrewsbury and that of the Wedgwoods at Maer Hall nearby, was remarkable. It was apparently a very happy one except for the death of his mother, Susannah, in 1817. Though the loss had a profound effect on the eight-year-old Charles, it was well compensated for by the motherly devotion of his three elder sisters, to such an extent that in later years he could barely remember his mother. His father, an autocratic and overbearing man, became more difficult after the loss of his wife, though he was kind to his children and Charles never spoke of him with anything but deep respect and affection. There was always an escape from the patriarchal sternness of The Mount in the more easy-going atmosphere of nearby Maer Hall with Uncle Jos and a multitude of cousins.

The Mount, the house in Shrewsbury where Charles Darwin was brought up

Maer Hall, the Wedgwood family home in Staffordshire

Charles was sent to board at Shrewsbury School shortly after his mother's death. He was totally unsuited to the classical education offered there and walked the short distance home whenever he could during evenings and weekends to collect specimens in the countryside or conduct chemical experiments in a garden shed – a pastime that earned him the school nickname 'Gas'. Charles's elder brother Erasmus (Eras) shared his interest in the natural world and practical experimentation. Though their interests later diverged, the two were personally close throughout their lives.

Edinburgh

Robert Darwin was not pleased with Charles's lack of application to his school work and, when Charles exchanged his passion for chemistry for that of game shooting at the age of 15, his father finally exploded saying, 'You care for nothing but shooting, dogs and rat-catching, and you will be a disgrace to yourself and all your family'. The Doctor removed Charles from school early and decided to send him to join his brother Eras at Edinburgh University where he too would study medicine.

Erasmus Darwin, Charles's elder brother

A nineteenth century anatomy class. Surgery was carried out without anaesthetic at this time

BELOW *Edinburgh University where Charles Darwin studied medicine for a year*

RIGHT *Christ's College, Cambridge*

With the appropriate letters of introduction, Charles and Eras enjoyed their situation as wealthy young gentlemen in an exciting new city. However, Charles soon lost interest in his medical studies, partly because of the barbarity of nineteenth-century surgery long before the days of anaesthetics. His main interest was still natural history – observing and collecting in a new environment and discussing current ideas on the subject with fellow students and academics. Charles therefore left Edinburgh after only eighteen months and his father determined that he should go to Cambridge University to study to become a clergyman.

Cambridge and respectability

Though Darwin had some scruples about declaring his belief in all the doctrines of the Church of England, he did like the thought of being a country clergyman. He went up to Cambridge early in 1828 after the Christmas vacation to take his place at Christ's College. It soon became clear that Darwin's character and interests were much more suited to this environment. Here he was able to pursue his beetle-collecting and 'herborising' along the College 'backs' in the company of like-minded students. His mentor, the Reverend Professor John Stevens Henslow, was to 'influence his career more than any other'. Darwin joined Henslow's field excursions and was impressed by his breadth of knowledge in every branch of natural history. He soon became known at Cambridge as 'the man who walks with Henslow'.

Despite his continued concentration on specimen-collecting and sport, Darwin found the genteel environment of Cambridge more conducive to study. He did well enough 'to gain a good place among the men who do not go in for honours', and came tenth in the list of successful graduates in 1831.

Cartoon of Darwin by a fellow undergraduate and beetle-collector, Albert Way

Paradise Scheme

Henslow encouraged Darwin to read Humboldt's *Personal Narrative* of his journey to South America via the Canary Islands (1799–1804). Darwin was inspired by the idea of travelling abroad to see the places Humboldt described and was fired with a 'burning zeal to add even the most humble contribution to the noble structure of natural science'. He spent his last term at Cambridge scheming with a few friends about a collecting expedition to Tenerife and even began to learn Spanish in anticipation. In further preparation, Darwin took up a study of geology, as Humboldt insisted it was an important subject for scientific travellers. Darwin persuaded Henslow to 'cram' him on the use of technical instruments and trigonometry in geological descriptions.

Henslow also arranged for Darwin to join the Reverend Professor Adam Sedgwick, Professor of Geology, on his usual summer field excursion to North Wales. After a week of close supervision and confirmation of his interpretation of some local geological structures, Darwin spent another week on his own. He then went on to Barmouth to join some University friends and, while there, he learned of the death of the friend with whom he had been planning his Tenerife expedition.

Arriving home at the Mount in August 1831 after this disappointing news, Darwin found a letter from Henslow waiting for him. The letter enclosed another from Professor Peacock, offering the opportunity of a voyage around the world.

John Stevens Henslow, lithograph by T H Maguire, 1849

LEFT *A box of beetles that belonged to Charles Darwin*

THE STRUGGLE TOWARDS EVOLUTION

Before Evolution

Aristotle (384–322 BC) engraved from a statue in Rome

CHARLES DARWIN'S GRANDFATHER, Erasmus (1731–1802), had published his own theory of the process of 'generation'. Others too had speculated about the potential of living things to change. Why then had the process still not really been explained? Why were Darwin's ideas so revolutionary?

By the time Darwin published *The Origin of Species*, the subject of 'transformation' was being widely debated. The word 'evolution' was not commonly used at this time in the way we use it today. Instead, scientists used the term 'transmutation'.

Most of the facts supporting Darwin's theory had been identified and discussed throughout the eighteenth and early nineteenth centuries, but their significance was not fully recognised until Darwin, with inspired insight, proposed an explanation. Thomas Henry Huxley, who championed Darwin's work for many years, could not understand why his theory had not been formulated before, nor indeed, why he had not thought of it himself.

One reason is that the traditional view of nature, dominated by Christian doctrine, was so deeply ingrained in Western culture that it remained essentially unchallenged. The general understanding of the place of mankind and animals in the universe was governed for many centuries by the idea of the Creation and the Great Chain of Being – a hierarchy of creatures with mankind at the top and simple organisms at the bottom. These plants and animals bred only with others of the same type and never changed their basic form.

The idea that living things could change or

Part of an illustration from Buffon's Histoire Naturelle, *one of the first books to suggest that changes in the natural world could occur by chance*

RIGHT *Garden of Eden from a Luther Bible c.1530*

give rise to forms different from themselves was considered heretical at the beginning of the nineteenth century, though it had been suggested time after time even by some of the Ancient Greek philosophers. Aristotle was interested in the development of living organisms, and Empedocles considered that, 'the creatures survived, being accidentally compounded in a suitable way; but where this did not happen, the creatures perished and are perishing still'.

The Received Wisdom

The English tradition of Creationism was evident in published works such as John Ray's *The Wisdom of God Manifested in the Works of*

Creation (1691). He did propose the concept of a species as a group of interbreeding organisms, but believed that they were 'unchangeable from the first'.

The Swedish naturalist, Linnaeus (1707-78), also believed that animals and plants were unchanged from the moment of creation. He introduced a system of categorising which is still the basis of the system we use today. For each species he provided a two-part name, the first indicating the group to which it is related and the second its unique identity; thus the edible oyster was given the Latin name *Ostrea edulis*.

At about the same time, the French naturalist, Comte de Buffon, was publishing his *Histoire Naturelle* which suggested that change could occur by environmental influences or simply by chance. However, he judiciously maintained that, 'all animals have participated equally in the grace of Creation'. Darwin acknowledged Buffon's contribution to his own ideas on the modification of species, but dismissed his opinions 'as he does not enter on the causes or means of transformation of species.'

Influences on Darwin

Another of the great French naturalists, J B Lamarck (1744-1829), was the most famous scientist to develop a theory of progressive change. He proposed that animals were continually changing by the gradual accumulation of acquired characteristics, so that succeeding generations were progressively more advanced than their ancestors. His theory was based on the idea of adaptation. His examples demonstrated a gradual progression of complexity that greatly influenced naturalists before Darwin.

Lamarck used the idea of spontaneous generation, or continuous creation of tiny bits of living matter. This explained the 'gaps' that would occur in the natural chain as the lowest orders of plants and animals struggled to become more advanced and moved up the chain.

Lamarck was strongly criticised by Georges Cuvier (1769-1832), who believed that when the earth experienced violent natural events such as floods or earthquakes, God replenished the stock of living things.

However, many fossils showed signs of variation from each other, as do living species, making naturalists argue about whether change was continuous or caused by isolated events.

It was therefore through geology that much of the story of life came to be explained. Charles Lyell developed the ideas of James Hutton (1726-97) that the physical processes of sedimentation, erosion and volcanic activity occurred in the past at about the same rate and frequency as they do at present, and rejected the Catastrophist interpretation of the formation of the earth. This 'Uniformitarian' concept provided the method by which Darwin could make sense of the geological structures he was later to describe. Darwin learnt a great deal from Lyell's book *The Principles of Geology* and they were to become close friends.

In 1844 an anonymously published book, entitled *Vestiges of the Natural History of the Creation*, caused a scandal in respectable society. The author, later revealed to be the journalist Robert Chambers, suggested, in bold language, the perpetual transformation of species. The book was immensely popular (it ran to eleven editions by 1860), and it excited those people longing for social reform. The scandal it created was undoubtedly one of the reasons why Charles Darwin, who had by 1844 completed the first draft of what was to be *The Origin of Species*, delayed publication for another fifteen years.

LEFT *The French naturalist Comte de Buffon*

ABOVE *The French naturalist, J B Lamarck*

BELOW *The geologist Charles Lyell was a close friend of Darwin's*

AWFUL CHANGES.
MAN FOUND ONLY IN A FOSSIL STATE.——REAPPEARANCE OF ICHTHYOSAURI.

A Lecture.—" You will at once perceive," continued PROFESSOR ICHTHYOSAURUS, "that the skull before us belonged to some of the lower order of animals; the teeth are very insignificant, the power of the jaws trifling, and altogether it seems wonderful how the creature could have procured food."

Professor Ichthyosaurus lectures on the unsuitability of Homo Sapiens for survival on the earth. Sir Henry de la Beche, Curiosities of Natural History, *1830*

A VOYAGE OF DISCOVERY

*The circumstances are
these:
Captain FitzRoy (a
nephew of the Duke of
Grafton's) sails at the end
of September in a ship to
survey in the first instance
the south coast of Tierra
del Fuego, afterwards to
visit the South Sea Islands
and to return by the
Indian Archipelago to
England: The expedition is
entirely for scientific
purposes and the ship will
generally wait your leisure
for researches in natural
history etc. Captain
FitzRoy is a public-
spirited and zealous officer
of delightful manners ...*

*Darwin's list of his father's
objections to him going on
the* Beagle *voyage*

RIGHT *A compass, used by
Darwin on the* Beagle

DARWIN RECOGNISED THE INVITATION
to join HMS *Beagle* on a surveying
'trip to Terra del Fuego and home by
the East Indies', as the opportunity of a lifetime.
A naturalist was needed but it was very
important to the captain, Robert FitzRoy, that
the gentleman concerned would be a suitable
travelling companion. Henslow considered
Darwin to be the best qualified person he knew
who was likely to undertake such an adventure.
He told Darwin that he had singled him out:

*'not on the supposition of yr. being a finished
Naturalist, but as amply qualified for collecting,
observing and noting anything worthy to be noted
in Natural History.'*

At first, Darwin's father strenuously objected
to the venture, but was soon persuaded by
'Uncle Jos' Wedgwood, who was full of
encouragement for the scheme.

Robert FitzRoy, Captain of the Beagle

for so long, and he was troubled by palpitations
which convinced him that he had heart disease.

The *Beagle* finally set sail on 27 December
1831, having twice been forced back to harbour
by violent storms. Darwin was not prepared for
the discomforts of life at sea and suffered
terribly from seasickness. For days at a time he
could eat only raisins and dry biscuits and lie
for hours in his cabin. However, when he began
to spend increasingly longer periods on shore,
up to four months on a couple of occasions, the
discomforts were more than compensated for by
the extraordinary experiences that
were to shape the rest of his life.

Having been denied the
opportunity to land at Tenerife,
Darwin's disappointment
evaporated once he reached the
Cape Verde Islands. As he
'rested beneath a low cliff,
with the sun glaring hot' he
was 'thrilled with delight' at

Captain FitzRoy's meticulous refitting of
the ship delayed their sailing by four
months during which Darwin packed and
repacked his tiny cabin with jars, books and
instruments including a new microscope. His
initial excitement was sometimes dampened
by the thought of leaving his family and friends

LEFT *Watercolour of the* Beagle *in the Murray Narrow, Tierra del Fuego by Conrad Martens*

RIGHT *A telescope owned by Darwin*

Title page and frontispiece of Lyell's Principles of Geology

the thought 'that I might perhaps write a book on the geology of the various countries visited'. Humboldt's inspiring descriptions of the volcanic landscape renewed his passion for geology, while Lyell's book on *The Principles of Geology* opened his mind to processes working to form the landscape. Almost daily, his experiences were magnified by Lyell's daring ideas, stirring him to ever greater excitement.

Every new landscape, from the exotic wonders of the tropical rain forest, to the arid pampas, mountain ranges and coral islands, stimulated Darwin to challenge existing ideas about the natural world. At this point he did not realise to what extent his experiences were leading to his later evolutionary theories, but he knew that he must diligently record all his observations in a series of field notebooks. Darwin also entered his impressions in his *Journal* throughout the five-year voyage and detailed his experiences in numerous letters sent home to family and friends. He amassed a huge collection of specimens, employing a sailor to help him skin and clean birds and mammals and sort and pack shells, plants, bones and rocks, which he shipped back to Henslow in Cambridge.

Although Darwin and Captain FitzRoy held differing views on many subjects, including politics and religion, they maintained a mutual respect that was essential for two men living in such close proximity for such a long time. Darwin, unaccustomed to shipboard discipline, was disturbed by the severity of the standard Navy punishment of flogging for wayward crew members. FitzRoy gently ridiculed Darwin for the piles of apparent rubbish he collected.

Darwin's friendly nature and great enthusiasm endeared him to the crew, several of whom, including Captain FitzRoy, were keen naturalists themselves. They admired Darwin's boundless energy on land and soon became active in helping him with his collections. As the philosophical member of the crew he earned the nickname 'Philos'.

The Midshipman's berth of a British frigate of the early nineteenth century painted by Augustus Earle, one of the Beagle's *artists. The* Beagle's *quarters would have been considerably more cramped than this*

The spectacular megatherium bones found by Darwin in S. America caused great excitement when they arrived in London

WELLCOME INSTITUTE LIBRARY, LONDON

Darwin's rock hammer

In Patagonia Darwin's sporting skills were enhanced by learning to use the bolas with which the gauchos caught the great birds called rheas. There he was told of another, rare ostrich, later described by John Gould and named in his honour, Rhea darwinii.

Part of a cross-section of the Andes, drawn by Charles Darwin

The Megatherium

One of Darwin's most exciting discoveries during the early part of the voyage, happened in September 1832. The *Beagle* rounded a headland called Punta Alta, near Bahia Blanca, about 400 miles south of Buenos Aires. In a low cliff Darwin spotted some bones and shells in the rock. Further investigation and a day's frenzied work with his servant Covington with pick axes, revealed them to be enormous fossil bones including a massive jaw bone containing a tooth. Darwin realised that this was part of the skeleton of the 'great antediluvial animal the Megatherium'. The significance of the find can only be appreciated with the knowledge that there was just one full specimen in Europe at this time and that extinction was a concept almost as revolutionary at the time as 'transmutation'.

The Andes

Some of Darwin's most revolutionary thinking was inspired by his expedition to the Andes mountains from Valparaiso in 1834. As he surveyed the breathtaking scenery of the high Andes during his 500-mile excursion to Copiapo, he found marine deposits incorporating the remains of a fossilised forest. Darwin became convinced that this part of the South American continent had at one time been under the sea before being raised more than 7,000 feet.

The volcanic eruptions they witnessed from near the island of Chiloe, and the earthquake which caused such devastation at Concepcion, showed Lyell's geological principles in action, leading Darwin to harbour 'ridiculous' thoughts that were more revolutionary than Lyell's own. The experience of these natural phenomena and the dramatic landscape had a profound effect not only on Darwin but also the rest of the crew and even on the hardened traveller Captain FitzRoy.

Trekking across the Andes was one of the most extraordinary experiences of Darwin's trip

During this expedition Darwin was taken seriously ill with a fever suggested to have been caused by the 'poisonous' Benchuga Bug. This must have been one of the frequent periods during the voyage when Darwin yearned for the affection of his family and the security of home. There was a constant flow of correspondence from his sisters, filled with news of family and Shropshire society, and also of the political situation which Darwin followed avidly. However, the letters were usually delayed by at least three months and Darwin must sometimes have felt very isolated.

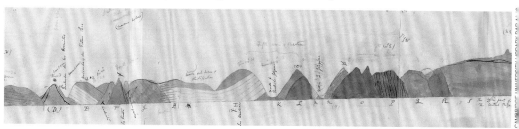

The Fuegians

Apart from Darwin, there were four other passengers on board the *Beagle* – three young Fuegians whom FitzRoy had earlier taken to England to educate and 'civilise', with the plan of returning them to spread Christianity and civilisation among their own people. He had named them York Minster, Fuegia Basket and Jemmy Button (whom he had bought for a button). With the Fuegians was Richard Matthews, from the Church Missionary Society.

The *Beagle* landed at Woolya, Tierra del Fuego, where Darwin was amazed by the experience of meeting wild, naked humans. He wrote,

'How entire the difference between wild and civilised man is. It is greater than between a wild and a domesticated animal.'

The three Fuegians were left with their original tribe, and a year later, the *Beagle* returned to the area where FitzRoy found Jemmy Button, once again naked with matted hair. He had to acknowledge that his experiment had failed.

Darwin was shocked by the primitive tribal life at Woolya Cove, Tierra del Fuego

The Galapagos Islands

After leaving the coast of South America, the *Beagle* headed west to the Galapagos Islands, home to a wonderful variety of animals including iguanas and giant tortoises. The Governor remarked that he could

tell from which island a tortoise came by the shape of its shell, and Darwin himself noticed a distinction between the mocking-thrushes in the sparse vegetation. When John Gould started to study and draw the finches after the voyage, it became apparent that they too were divided up among the islands, each kind appropriate to the food and conditions it found there.

The South Pacific and Home

The essential work of the voyage complete, the *Beagle* turned south across the Pacific to Tahiti, New Zealand and Australia and then to the Indian Ocean. It was there in the Keeling (or Cocos) Islands that Darwin was able to study the 'gardens of brilliantly coloured coral'. From these observations and previous ones, he began to consolidate his ideas about coral formations.

The homeward journey passed via Cape Town to St Helena, where Darwin saw Napoleon's tomb and then to Ascension Island. To complete his circumnavigation, FitzRoy returned to the coast of South America. The *Beagle* landed at Falmouth on 2 October 1836.

The variations between the tortoises on the Galapagos Islands was a major factor in causing Darwin to later reflect on the possibility of the 'transmutation' of species

Illustration of the three Fuegians on board the Beagle

FROM DARWIN'S AUTOBIOGRAPHY:

'The voyage of the Beagle has been by far the most important event in my life and has determined my whole career ... I have always felt that I owe to the Voyage the first real training or education of my mind.

A land iguana. An illustration from the Zoology of the Beagle *(1838–42)*

23

RETURN FROM THE VOYAGE AND LIFE IN LONDON

DARWIN DID NOT LINGER ON THE *Beagle* after it docked in Falmouth but made straight for Shropshire and home. During the two-day coach drive, he felt 'that the wide world does not contain so happy a prospect as the rich cultivated land of England'.

Darwin's father and three sisters were delighted to see him. Though he enjoyed the attention lavished on him, domestic details seemed trivial and ten days after landing, Darwin was back with Henslow in Cambridge, catching up with the news and being introduced to people who might be able to take his collections.

There was no doubt that Darwin's voyage had changed him. People found him more confident and he had a new purpose in life. He was no longer interested in being a clergyman but had earned the approval of the scientific community and of his father.

The reality of life in England, even from Darwin's privileged vantage point, was perplexing. The new Poor Law was causing bitter resentment. The underlying philosophy of the Act was based on the Malthusian principle of natural 'checks' as a means of controlling overpopulation. Malthus's ideas were later to have a profound effect on Darwin's scientific thinking. Workhouses were being built and there had been riots in the southern counties in May 1835. Darwin (a Whig supporter) felt his strong political awareness, less relevant while at sea, returning. He wrote to FitzRoy that 'by the time we meet, my politics will be as firmly fixed and wisely founded as ever'.

London

After five days in Cambridge, Darwin moved on to London, and arrived at the home of his brother Erasmus. He was overwhelmed by the bustling city but found that he was already a celebrity. His 'Megatherium' bones from Patagonia had been displayed at the 1833 meeting of the British Association, and the little-known species had caused quite a stir. Darwin was courted by some of London's most influential scientists and thinkers and was introduced to his hero, author of the *Principles of Geology* and President of the Geological Society,

Poverty was widespread in the mid-nineteenth century and many workhouses were opening

The library at the Athenaeum Club of which Darwin was a member

A meeting of the Geological Society of London

The Galapagos finches, drawn by John Gould for the Zoology of the Beagle

Charles Lyell. Lyell introduced him to others including Richard Owen, Professor of Anatomy at the Royal College of Surgeons. Darwin was proposed for membership of the Geological Society and elected to the Athenaeum Club (at the same time as Charles Dickens).

Darwin's real debut in the scientific world was his presentation to the Geological Society on 4 January 1837 of his paper entitled *Proofs of recent elevation on the coast of Chile*. Lyell was in the audience and the paper made a great impression.

Finding naturalists to examine and write about the material he had collected proved a more difficult task than Darwin had anticipated, but to his surprise the British Treasury agreed to give at least some of the financial assistance necessary and he managed to find various experts to take on the different groups of animals – birds, fish and reptiles, mammals and fossil mammals. He was left with the rocks and minerals, invertebrates and plants to record himself. Though he decided he would have to stay in 'dirty, odious London' for some years to further his work, he first went to Cambridge for three months to deal with the collection and to work on the *Journal of Researches*, based on the daily journal written during the *Beagle* voyage. During a visit to the Wedgwood home, Maer Hall, Darwin was encouraged to tell endless tales of his adventures and to begin writing up his notes. The *Journal* was finished in London and became the third volume of a set FitzRoy produced about the circumnavigation. The *Zoology of the Voyage of the Beagle* was published separately and Darwin continued to work on the *Geology*.

On his return to London, Darwin took lodgings in Great Marlborough Street near his brother Erasmus who entertained the elite of London society at the time. Darwin went out and about with the sociable Lyell. He frequented the Athenaeum Club and the home of Harriet Martineau, the great social reformer, who was an intimate friend of Erasmus. Darwin also tried to find time for some general reading, particularly the work of his favourite poet, Milton, and that of Coleridge and Wordsworth.

In July 1837 Darwin secretly opened his first notebook on the transmutation of species (later to be called evolution) and began scribbling down his ideas, testing out the theory of progressive change. At this time he had not thought of natural selection. He sketched an irregularly branching tree to illustrate his idea of a family history for the animals, with the trunk symbolising their common ancestry.

Darwin's work on this notebook and the others that followed coincided with recurrences of the palpitations he had suffered before embarking on the voyage. It seems likely that deteriorations in his health often recurred in Darwin's life during periods of great stress, especially when forcing himself to consider his heretical ideas on transmutation.

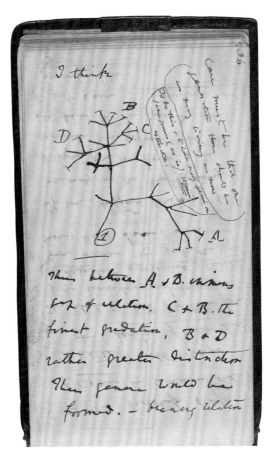

ABOVE *Some pill boxes of Darwin's, later used for specimens*

LEFT *A page of Darwin's 'transmutation' notebook showing the famous 'branching tree' sketch – Darwin's first attempt at illustrating his theory*

'MARRY, MARRY, MARRY!'

RIGHT *Emma Darwin and Charles Darwin. Chalk and water-colour drawings by George Richmond*

DURING HIS YEARS IN LONDON, Darwin often thought of the countryside. Having travelled the world, he now found himself in an increasingly dirty, overcrowded city. His thoughts began to turn more frequently towards marriage and, true to his analytical nature, Darwin drew up a balance sheet listing the advantages and disadvantages of matrimony. The odds came down heavily on the side of marriage. He wrote:

'My God, it is intolerable to think of spending one's whole life like a neuter bee living all one's days solitarily in smoky, dirty London. Only picture to yourself a nice soft wife on a sofa, with a good fire and books and music perhaps – compare this vision with the dingy reality of Gt. Marboro' St ... Marry, Marry, Marry! Q.E.D.'

Darwin had become very attached to his first cousin, Emma Wedgwood, the daughter of his Uncle Jos, whom he had seen regularly since childhood. She seemed to combine all the qualities he desired in a wife and, with some paternal advice, he chose and was accepted by her. His sister Caroline had married Emma's brother Jos two years earlier and this new marriage brought equal delight to both families.

Emma, like Charles, was thirty years old when they married on 29 January 1839. She was well educated and independent in spirit. She knew French, Italian and German and was an excellent needlewoman. Her main accomplishment however was as a pianist and she continued to play regularly until the end of her life. To her family, Emma was known as 'little Miss Slip-Slop' because of her disorderliness, and she wrote that she appreciated Charles for 'not being fastidious'.

Emma was totally devoted to Charles and willingly adapted her life to the demands of his constant illness and his work. Just after accepting his marriage proposal she wrote of him:

'He is the most open transparent man I ever saw, and every word expresses his real thoughts. He is particularly affectionate and very nice to his father and sisters, and perfectly sweet-tempered ...'

The one subject that might have divided them seems not to have done so. Emma was sincerely religious, as were most of her family, and Darwin's ideas were inherently challenging to her faith. Despite this she always agreed to

The 'balance sheet' drawn up by Darwin to help him weigh up the advantages and disadvantages of marriage

read Darwin's manuscripts before he sent them on to scientific friends and helped further his work in every way she could.

Darwin and Emma were married in Staffordshire in 1839. They took a house in Upper Gower Street, London, which they called 'Macaw Cottage' because of its brightly-coloured decor. Social demands competed with Darwin's scientific work; and within the year his attention was further diverted by the birth of their first child, William Erasmus. This new adventure was met with all the enthusiasm of the tropical explorer. Darwin recorded his observations of his 'little animalcule of a son' and showed him a degree of affection completely at odds with the stereotype of the distant Victorian father figure. One of the traits that Emma and others found appealing in Darwin was his tenderness towards his children.

As on so many occasions to follow, life at this time was marred by Darwin's illness. The symptoms of stomach complaints and headaches were often too severe for him to work.

A 'Theory by which to work'

Perhaps stimulated by all the talk of Malthusian principles, the new Poor Law and Christian morality, Darwin read Malthus's *Essay on the Principles of Population*. Its implications for his own theory made a powerful impact on him and, nearly forty years later, in his autobiography he wrote that, 'being well prepared to appreciate the struggle for existence which everywhere goes on from long continued observation of the habits of animals and plants, it at once struck me that under these circumstances favourable variations would tend to be preserved and unfavourable ones destroyed. The results of this would be the formation of new species. Here, then I had at last got a theory by which to work.'

The rest of Darwin's life was to be devoted to amassing evidence to support his theory.

In March 1841 the Darwins' second child, Anne Elizabeth was born, providing her father with as much joy as her brother, plus added anxiety and again, worsening of the symptoms of his illness. The thought of moving out of London was never far from Darwin's mind and it seems that, consciously or unconsciously, he was eager to withdraw from the demands of society, both social and scientific.

During the early summer of 1842 Darwin wrote out a brief sketch of his Species theory. He had by then accumulated sufficient material to feel confident about what he referred to as a 'natural means of selection'. He had also sent the Coral Reefs part of the *Geology of the Voyage* to the publishers.

Emma was expecting their third child and Macaw Cottage was becoming inadequate for the growing family and their servants. Dr Darwin had agreed to help meet the cost of a house in the country and they decided that this was the time to move.

The site of Macaw Cottage – the London house lived in by Charles and Emma Darwin when they married

LEFT *Darwin and his son William in an early daguerrotype*

Cross-section through a coral reef, drawn by Darwin to illustrate its formation by subsidence

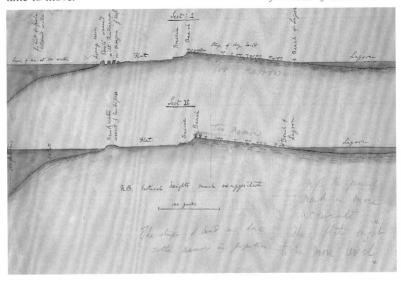

THE MOVE TO DOWN

AFTER SEVERAL FRUITLESS SEARCHES in Surrey and elsewhere, the Darwins settled on a 'property about a quarter of a mile from the small village of Downe in Kent'. At first they intended to rent the house for a year, but accepted the very favourable purchase price of £2200. Emma moved on 14 September 1842 and Darwin followed a few days later.

Their third child, Mary Eleanor, was born just a few days after the move on 23 September but sadly died only three weeks later. The first few months at Down were therefore miserable ones for the family, made worse by the illness of Emma's father, Josiah Wedgwood. Darwin reacted in his characteristic way and threw himself into his work to forget his grief.

Downe (the 'e' was added shortly before the Darwins moved there but they did not wish to change the spelling of the house) was a small village of about 40 houses, mainly inhabited by tenant farmers and agricultural labourers. The George and Dragon Inn and the church stood, as they do now, at the centre of the village. Darwin wrote to his sister Catty:

'The little pot-house where we slept [overnight while viewing the house] is a grocers-shop and the landlord is the carpenter – so you may guess style of village... A carrier goes weekly to London and calls anywhere for anything in London, and takes anything anywhere.'

House improvements and garden schemes

Down House was, in 1842, a squarish Georgian building not unlike Darwin's childhood home, the Mount, in Shrewsbury, with domestic offices and outbuildings. It was set in about 18 acres of land including a meadow and an orchard. It was not their ideal choice – Emma did not much like it at first and Darwin described it as '... ugly, looks neither old nor new'. To Darwin however, the joy of being once again in the countryside was so great that it overcame any other considerations and, again with the financial help of his father, they were able to afford to alter the house and grounds extensively to suit their needs.

Downe Village c.1900

Wood Anemone.

'*The charm of the place to me is that almost every field is intersected (as alas is ours) by one or more footpaths – I never saw so many walks in any other country. The country is extraordinarily rural and quiet with narrow lanes and high hedges and hardly any ruts. It is really surprising to think London is only 16 miles off.*'

The first of the many improvements was the construction of a three-storey bay to the back of the house to give more elegantly proportioned rooms and panoramic views of the garden.

The rebuilding of the servants' wing in 1845 included the construction of a school room and two small bedrooms on the first floor above the remodelled kitchen, butler's hall and new back door. The house was extended twice more to provide even better accommodation for Darwin's growing family and its needs, including eventually seven children, a cook, servants, butler, governess and children's nurse and room for the scores of guests who visited – principally Emma's family.

Plans for the garden

As soon as he saw it, Darwin began to scheme about the garden. One of the earliest projects was to increase the privacy of the house by moving and lowering the lane, which ran along the boundary towards the village, by about two feet – a huge building task for any private owner. This provided enough topsoil to create a bank along the northern frontage of the house on which a flint and brick wall was constructed.

This afforded shelter from the cold prevailing winds and much more privacy. Soon they were 'undertaking some [more] great earthworks; making a new walk in the [kitchen] garden; and removing the mound under the Yews'. Darwin had bought an additional piece of land to the north, known as The Slip, through which his access drive ran. A new mound was constructed 'in front of the door out of the house [to the north], between two of the lime trees.'

The Sandwalk

Darwin purchased a strip of land about 300 yards long that bordered the western boundary of his field. He fenced it and planted 'underwood, shrubs and trees', expanding the broad hedgerow into a wood. The heavy clay surface was dressed with sand and thus Darwin called it his Sandwalk. He kept a pile of flints by the side of the path at the start of his walk and would kick one off each time he made a complete round.

Within only a couple of years of their occupation, Down House began to acquire much of the character that can be seen today. Darwin had every reason to go ahead with the alterations as soon as possible as he had already decided that this location and lifestyle were never to change for the rest of his life. He wrote in a letter to Captain FitzRoy:

LEFT *Family group outside the bay window of the Dining Room. From left to right: Leonard, Etty, Horace, Emma, Bessy, Frank and an unknown visitor*

RIGHT *A walking stick belonging to Darwin*

'My life goes on like clockwork and I am fixed on the spot where I shall end it.'

Darwin easily acquired the role (to which he had been brought up) of country gentleman. He launched instinctively into the detail of what price his hay could fetch and how to build a container to hold liquid manure for use in the garden. He personally supervised all the alterations:

'I was called off yesterday to speak to workmen at 9 o'clock and excepting an hour's rest on the sofa at luncheon time, I was on my legs till 5 o'clock: this is the way I pass most days and am too much knocked up in the evenings'

(27 APRIL 1843, TO SUSAN DARWIN)

Parish and civic duty

In the early years of his residence at Down Darwin concentrated his energies on his work, his family and the extensive alterations to Down House and its grounds. Only later did he take on the involvement in parish affairs that some might have felt his status in the village demanded. In 1852 he became one of the founders of the Downe Friendly Society or 'Coal Club', and served as its Treasurer for thirty years. The Club's Annual General Meeting was held at Down House, usually on Whit Monday. Another member of the 'Coal Club', Sir John Lubbock of the neighbouring High Elms estate, a banker with scientific

interests, encouraged Darwin to accept the honorary position of Magistrate in the Petty Sessions Court at Bromley. Darwin attended the court regularly but, like other demands on his time, hearing cases quite exhausted him.

Emma ran the Sunday School and taught village children to read. She also visited the poorer members of the community, taking them food and medicines.

Darwin's account books for the household expenses for the period show the names of many local families still living in the village who supplied the house with beer, coal, groceries, animal feeds and labour. All the alterations and building works, for example, were carried out by John Lewis, the carpenter, and Isaac Lazlett.

A watercolour of Down House in 1880 by Albert Goodwin

A MAN OF LETTERS

Postcard from Charles Darwin to Alfred Russel Wallace (who put forward a theory of transmutation very similar to Darwin's own)

A set of small drawers in Darwin's study

Isolation but not isolated

ONE OF THE MAIN REASONS DARWIN was attracted to Downe was that despite its 'extreme quietness and rusticity' it was only 16 miles (26km) from central London. He intended to spend a night or two in London every month 'to keep up my communications with scientific men' and 'not turn into a complete Kentish hog'. Despite these good intentions, the difficult carriage drive down eight miles of country lanes to Sydenham or Croydon railway station and Darwin's constant ill-health, meant that he was not able to visit London or friends and family elsewhere nearly as often as he had planned. He wrote to Captain FitzRoy:

'I find most unfortunately for myself, that the little excitement of breaking out of my most quiet routine so generally knocks me up, that I am able to do scarcely anything when in London, and I have not even been able to attend one evening meeting of the Geological Society.'

(TO CAPT. FITZROY, 31 MARCH 1843)

Darwin did, however, continue his 'communications with scientific men' through a prolific correspondence with a wide range of people.

Letter-writing was part of the daily routine into which Darwin's life soon settled. He revelled in the relative isolation of Down which meant that each day could be spent quietly, working away in his study or in quiet pursuits in the midst of his family.

The lifelong correspondence with his cousin William Darwin Fox, probably Darwin's closest friend, began in their student days when it largely concerned beetle-collecting. Other longer-term correspondences were begun during the *Beagle* voyage when letter-writing was Darwin's only means of communication. Darwin kept up a constant flow of letters to his friends and family and wrote to his sister Susan:

'how entirely the pleasure in arriving in a new place depends on letters.'

He began to exchange letters with the geologists Sedgwick and Charles Lyell and kept up a friendship and corrrespondence with Lyell throughout his life. Another lifelong friend and sympathetic scientist was Joseph Hooker, the Director of Kew Gardens, with whom Darwin exchanged perhaps 1400 letters. From these letters we can not only trace the development of Darwin's ideas but can also gain a good impression of natural scientific thought for much of the Victorian era.

Another favourite correspondent was T H Huxley who was to champion Darwin's theory and did much to professionalise science during the period.

Gathering information

The main content of Darwin's letters during any given period would revolve around his particular area of study at the time, and he tirelessly sought out the people who were most likely to provide useful information. He often wrote to other authors or to magazines commenting on various articles. He set up a correspondence with *The Gardeners' Chronicle* about a wide range of botanical topics, sought readers' advice and set up various experiments. He wrote to Miles Berkeley about his experiments with hybridising peas, and to Hooker at Kew with all manner of queries.

Much of the information Darwin gathered through his letters was stored away as evidence to support his 'species' theory and Darwin acknowledged many of his correspondents in his book *On the Origin of Species*. During his long life Darwin probably wrote in the region of 7000 letters.

TO CAROLINE DARWIN, 6 DECEMBER 1826, FROM EDINBURGH

'My dear Caroline,
Many thanks for your very entertaining letter, which was a great relief after hearing a long stupid lecture from Duncan on Materia Medica.... Dr Duncan is so very learned that his wisdom has left no room for his sense ...'

LETTER TO W D FOX, 30 JUNE 1828
FROM SHREWSBURY

' you cannot conceive with what great pleasure I look out for an Entom. Letter now that I have nobody to talk to.'
(FROM SAME LETTER):
'Fig: (I) is this a Cychrus? I make it so by Lamarck. (NB when you recognise an insect by my description always say whether you possess it)...
Taken in plenty, the little beetle that destroys Scotch firs. What is its name.'

William Darwin Fox was a close friend and correspondent of Darwin's from childhood

FROM CATHERINE DARWIN, 26-27 APRIL 1832

'Erasmus left us today; he told me to send you his love and to tell you that he did not write to you, as you and he had come to an understanding not to write to each other, and that Brothers never could write to each other. Erasmus talks with the greatest interest for your letters and says "how grand it makes him feel and how strange it is, actually to have a Brother in South America."'

FROM CAROLINE, 12 MARCH 1832, FROM MAER

'We are in daily hopes of a letter from Madeira as it is high time we calculate for a letter and we are getting very impatient my dear Tactus to hear from you – I mean to fill this letter very much with Maer news.'

TO JOSEPH HOOKER, 15 JANUARY 1861

'My dear Hooker
The sight of your hand-writing always rejoices the very cockles of my heart –. I most fully agree to what you say about Huxley's article and power of writing.
What a smasher for Owen!
The whole Review seems to me excellent ...
Have you read Woman in White ... the plot is wonderfully interesting ... I am very glad to hear so good an account of Mrs Hooker and your children ...'

Joseph Dalton Hooker (Director of Kew Gardens) became a good friend of Darwin's after he returned from an Antarctic exploring voyage

FROM SUSAN DARWIN, 12 FEBRUARY 1832

'I have one more marriage to finish up with, but nothing very interesting: your charming cousin Lucy Galton is engaged to marry Mr Mailliet: the eldest son of a very fat Mrs Mailliet who was once here ... As I have no new Direction I must take my chance at Rio de Janeiro.'

'Darwin in his study' by the Russian artist Evstafieff

FROM JEFFRIES WYMAN, 8 JANUARY 1861 (FROM CAMBRIDGE, MASSACHUSSETS).

'My Dear Sir,
It gives me great pleasure to answer insofar as I am able, your enquiries with regard to the rattlesnake.'

TO THE GARDENERS' CHRONICLE, (BEFORE 5 JANUARY 1861.)

'Mr James Drummond sent me a packet of seeds of this plant from Swan River with the following memorandum: 'The achenia of several small composite plants, ... are blown about by the wind...'

WORK AND PLAY

The daily routine

Photograph of Darwin in about 1857

Some of the objects that can still be seen in Darwin's study

DARWIN WOULD RISE FAIRLY EARLY and go out for a walk before breakfast. From about 8.00am he would work in his study for an hour and a half, when he would take a break perhaps to listen to Emma reading family letters. He would then return to work until mid-day and after that, regardless of the weather, would take his daily stroll around the Sandwalk, usually accompanied by his dog. Lunch, the main meal of the day, was normally served at about one o'clock. He read the newspaper, wrote letters or read until 3.00pm, then he would rest, often listening to Emma read. At about 4.30pm he would resume work for an hour until 5.30pm when he would take another rest. A simple tea was served at 7.30pm, followed by a couple of games of backgammon with Emma, or listening to Emma playing the piano or reading to him.

Darwin's poor health was an increasing threat to his routine and each day would be adapted to the relative severity of his symptoms.

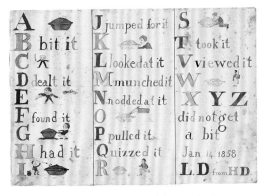

An alphabet from Horace Darwin's scrapbook

The children

Despite his constant work and his illness, Darwin's children remembered him as having infinite patience and kindness. Though he was often very absorbed in his work, Darwin never reprimanded the children for disturbing him. They were allowed to romp noisily around the house and even to go into the study for things they needed. Henrietta wrote:

'Another mark of his unbounded patience, was the way in which we were suffered to make raids into the study when we had an absolute need of sticking-plaster, string, pins, scissors, stamps, foot-rule, or hammer. I remember his patient look when he said once, "Don't you think you could not come in again, I have been interrupted very often."'

He took a great personal interest in all of them and played with them whenever he could. Henrietta also wrote:

'he always made us feel that we were each of us creatures whose opinions and thoughts were valuable to him, so that whatever there was best in us came out in the sunshine of his presence.'

Another child with happy memories of the Darwin household was Darwin's grand-daughter, Gwen Raverat, daughter of his son George.

In her book, *Period Piece* (1952), she describes the special atmosphere of Down and the happy times she spent there. She felt that the Darwin family was so close that, as adults, the children found it difficult to move away and be independent. She says:

'... to us, everything at Down was perfect. That was an axiom. And by us I mean not only the children, but all the uncles and aunts who belonged there. Uncle Horace was once heard to say in a surprised voice: "No, I don't really like salvias very much, though they did grow at Down."

The implication to us would have been obvious. Of course all the flowers that grew at Down were beautiful; and different from all other flowers.'

'The mulberry tree by the nursery window' from Period Piece – a Cambridge Childhood, *written by Darwin's grand-daughter, the artist Gwen Raverat*

The 'will'

In the summer of 1844 Darwin enlarged the brief sketch of his evolution theory to 230 pages. He was still reluctant to publish – thoughts of the possible reaction to an account of a godless origin of species made it too frightening to contemplate. Therefore, aware of his deteriorating health, he bundled the completed manuscript together and wrote an extraordinary letter to Emma – almost a will – including the specification of a sum of £400 to cover the cost of publication in the event of his 'sudden death'.

However, he felt that the theory was not quite complete, that he had:

An extract of the 'will' Darwin drew up instructing Emma on what to do with his Species *theory should he die before publishing it*

'overlooked one problem of great importance ... the tendency in organic beings descended from the same stock to diverge in character as they become modified.'

The solution to this problem came to him one day while riding in his carriage close to home. He later wrote in his autobiography:

'The solution, as I believe, is that the modified offspring of all dominant and increasing forms tend to become adapted to many and highly diversified places in the economy of nature.'

This, finally, was the crux of his argument - the idea of natural selection or 'the survival of the fittest'.

Page 3

A ray of the sun came to the moon & they jumped on the ray & away they slithered up to the sun, when they got to the sun the trees had no leaves because it was so boiling hot. The birds had hairs instead of feathers. The flowers, instead of petals, had feathers & inside of the flowers were little grinning faces grinning at you.

ABOVE *A fairy tale written by one of Darwin's children on the back of a page of his* Species *notes*

CENTRE *A train drawn by one of Darwin's children*

LEFT *A page from the* Species *notes*

BARNACLES AND BREEDING PIGEONS

Accumulating facts

IN AN EFFORT TO TAKE HIS MIND OFF the wider implications of his Species theory, Darwin concentrated his energy on a vigorously detailed study of barnacles using material and evidence gathered during his voyage. He agreed with Hooker that 'no one has hardly a right to examine the question of species who has not minutely described many.'

His *Geological Observations on South America* was ready for publication by October 1846 and he was able to turn his full attention to the curious little barnacle he had found off the coast of Chile, imbedded in the shell of a limpet-like rock snail. Darwin was convinced that this barnacle was unique and began to look closely at its structure and relationship with the other barnacles.

One of Darwin's microscopes

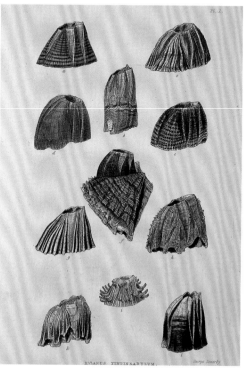

A colour plate from Darwin's 'barnacle book', a monograph on the sub-class Cirripedia, *the result of many years of work*

Progress was interrupted by the death of his father in November 1848 and the subsequent further deterioration of his own health.

The health spa at Malvern where Darwin went with his family to seek relief from his ailments

The water cure

The symptoms of Darwin's undiagnosed stomach complaint became so bad that some days he suffered from constant vomiting and could barely work at all. He wrote that he feared four-fifths of his time was wasted by illness and he became very preoccupied with thoughts of death.

When a friend recommended that he try the fashionable 'water cure', Darwin took his entire family to Dr James Gully's hydropathic establishment at Malvern, Worcestershire. The treatments, which many saw as 'quackery', were based on cold water being applied to the body to stimulate the circulation. Gully prescribed a strict routine and homoeopathic medicines three times a day which Darwin records taking obediently 'without an atom of faith'. He meant to be away for only six weeks but either the treatment or the escape from his work did make him feel much better. The whole family enjoyed the holiday and eventually stayed for four months.

From this point onwards, Darwin added a cold shower and morning scrub in the garden to his daily routine and believed that this did make him feel somewhat better.

'A bitter and cruel loss'

During the summer of 1850, the Darwins' eldest daughter Annie started to show signs of what Darwin feared was an inherited stomach disorder. Through the autumn and winter her condition deteriorated, and in late March, 1851, it was decided that she should go to Malvern. Darwin took Annie and her sister, Henrietta, with their nurse and governess, leaving Emma, who was eight months pregnant, at Down with the other children. Darwin returned to Down, but by mid-April Annie's condition became serious. He hurried back to Malvern but she died after only a few days. Darwin had enjoyed a particularly close relationship with Annie and he felt that he would never recover from his 'bitter & cruel loss'. It is often said that Annie's death was an important factor in Darwin's turning away from Christianity.

Even the Great Exhibition at Hyde Park provided only a minor diversion from the family's grief. However, Emma's safe delivery of another son, Horace, raised their spirits somewhat. Slowly Darwin resumed his barnacle work and it was to be his chief labour until 1854. The family became so accustomed to their father retiring to his study for hours at a time to pore over this work that one of the boys was once heard to ask a friend, 'Where does *your* Father do his barnacles?'

From barnacles to breeding birds

The barnacles clearly showed wide variation and novelty: each species or form adapted to its environment. But Darwin was eager to move on to another area of study to provide yet more evidence for his theory – that of domestication of animals and plants and the breeding of fancy forms. This was a popular pastime of the period and Darwin wrote scores of letters to farmers and gardeners encouraging them to send him the results of their experiments.

He turned his attention to the study of variation in fancy pigeons and was soon immersed in the world of pigeon-fancying, drinking at the clubs and picking up the jargon and gossip. This was most unusual for a gentleman scientist but Darwin was not content with recording what others did. He built a pigeon-house in the garden, bought all kinds of pigeons and soon began to breed them himself, afterwards boiling them in order to measure the differences in their skeletons. Darwin was in constant correspondence with other fanciers, and parcels would arrive daily containing pigeon corpses in various stages of decomposition. These, and the pit of pigeons' innards in the garden, finally made Darwin realise that Down was turning into a 'chamber of horrors', and he decided to send the birds out to be skeletonised professionally.

However, Darwin had achieved his aim of seeing at first hand the minute variations in form which the fanciers exploited to create pouters, fantails and tumblers. This confirmed Darwin's belief that similar imperceptible differences between other animals were selected in the natural world.

ABOVE *Breeding 'fancy' pigeons was a favourite pastime in Victorian times*

LEFT *Darwin spent some time in the unfamiliar world of the pigeon-fanciers' clubs. Illustration from the* Illustrated London News *(1853)*

THE ORIGIN OF SPECIES

Alfred Russel Wallace who formulated a theory similar to Darwin's own

IN 1855 LYELL RECOMMENDED TO DARWIN a paper, *On the Law which has regulated the Introduction of New Species*, by a comparatively unknown naturalist and collector, Alfred Russel Wallace. It showed a few similarities to his own theory. Darwin read it with interest, but noted 'nothing very new, … it all seems Creation with him'. Lyell had been urging him to prepare a summary of his theory for publication, fearing that someone else might do so before him, but Darwin did not see Wallace's ideas as a threat. Like Darwin, Wallace went travelling, and pursued his ideas as he collected specimens in the Malay Archipelago. While recovering from malaria in 1858 he reflected, as Darwin had done twenty years earlier, on Malthus's *Essay on Population*.

Wallace came to the same conclusion as Darwin: that natural selection was the factor controlling population size. He wrote his essay, *On the tendency of varieties to depart indefinitely from the original type*, and sent it to Darwin.

Darwin, Lyell and Hooker at Down House. A scene recreated by Evstafieff

Pain and frustration

When Darwin received Wallace's essay on 18 June 1858, he was very shocked. He thought that Wallace's ideas were identical to his own. He wrote to Lyell:

'Your words have come true with a vengeance that I should be forestalled … I never saw a more striking coincidence, if Wallace had my M.S. Sketch written out in 1842 he could not have made a better short abstract! Even his terms now stand as Heads of my Chapters.'

If Darwin had looked a little more closely at the manuscript, he would have seen that it differed from his own in some essential elements but his response was unlikely to be a calm one.

The timing of the shock could not have been worse for Darwin as two of his children were seriously ill. His daughter Henrietta was recovering from suspected diphtheria and their youngest child, Charles, became mortally ill with scarlet fever and died only days later.

Darwin was desperate to decide whether it was right to try to publish before Wallace or whether to allow Wallace to publish first. The thought of his life's work being in vain was devastating to Darwin but at the same time he was so preoccupied with concern and grief for his children that he was unable to act.

He wrote to Hooker on 29 June:

'I am quite prostrated and can do nothing but I send Wallace and my abstract of my letter to Asa Gray …[and] my sketch of 1844 … I really cannot bear to look at it. Do not waste much time. It is miserable in me to care at all about priority.'

Lyell and Hooker, who were determined to do what they could to save Darwin from being forestalled, persuaded him to prepare a joint

LEFT *Emma Darwin with her son Leonard in about 1854*

FAR LEFT *Darwin's daughter Henrietta as a young woman (1865)*

paper with Wallace that could be presented at a meeting of the Linnean Society. Luckily an extra meeting of the Society was fitted in before the summer recess and the paper was read on 1 July 1858.

Wallace did not know that a reading of his essay had been planned, and there was not enough time to contact him before the day. However, when he was told, he was very generous about the situation and said that all the real work had been done by Darwin.

Ironically, the announcement of 'the very ingenious theory to account for the appearance and perpetuation of varieties and of specific forms' caused little excitement at the time. Few realised the significance of what they were hearing. During the meeting Darwin remained at Downe where he was burying his son Charles in the parish churchyard. He therefore had little time to dwell on the announcement of his theory.

The outbreak of scarlet fever in Downe village looked dangerously like an epidemic and, somewhat belatedly, Darwin sent all the remaining children, except for Henrietta, to stay with Emma's sister, Elizabeth, in Sussex. Charles, Emma and Etty joined them and within the week they all travelled on to the Isle of Wight.

Out of danger from infection and at a safe distance from London and the reaction to his work, Darwin corrected his proofs for the Linnean Society's Proceedings and carried on his correspondence. He then began to prepare 'an abstract of [his] Species Theory'.

By the time the family returned to Downe in August 1858, Darwin was deeply involved in writing *On the Origin of Species*. It took him

thirteen months of working for several hours every day in his study.

The 'Theory' is published

The manuscript was eventually finished by mid-March 1859, and Darwin took Lyell's advice to approach John Murray to publish the book. Murray agreed even before he had seen the manuscript. Darwin's closest friends read and commented upon the draft manuscript. The title was settled and *On the Origin of Species by means of Natural Selection or the Preservation of Favoured Races in the Struggle for Life* was published in November 1859.

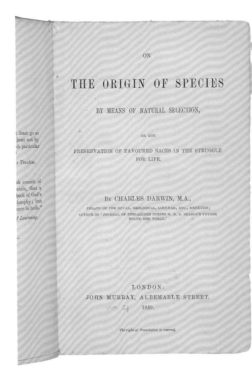

The title page and spine of the first edition of On the Origin of Species, *published in 1859*

THE BOOK THAT SHOOK THE WORLD

A colour lithograph cartoon of Darwin from Vanity Fair *(1871)*

RIGHT *Cartoon of Richard Owen, 'Old Bones', from* Vanity Fair

THOUGH IT IS ACCLAIMED AS ONE OF the great classics of scientific literature, Charles Darwin's *Origin of Species* was written in a way that can be understood by a wide general audience.

Darwin's theory is based on observable facts. It was the way in which he related them to each other that made it so unexpectedly different and valuable. The basis of his theory was that:

1. Species are made up of variable populations.
2. Variation is maintained by sexual reproduction.
3. Individuals produce more eggs or seeds than are needed for the species to survive.
4. Individuals that are well adapted to their environment will be more likely to survive and reproduce, thereby passing on their traits to succeeding generations.

The cumulative effect is 'descent with modification'.

Darwin wrote to T H Huxley that he was:

'intensely curious to hear what effect the book produces' knowing 'that there will be much in it which [he would] object to; … but if on the whole, you and two or three others think I am on the right road, I shall not care what the mob of naturalists think'.

On the Origin of Species was published on 24 November 1859. John Murray, the publisher, received orders for 1500 copies as soon as the book was released, two days before its official publication date. He therefore immediately asked Darwin to prepare a second edition. The most notable amendment to the first edition was in the final passage, where Darwin felt obliged to insert the reference to 'the Creator', to lessen the offence to his Christian readers.

The Origin was revised many times for subsequent editions. Darwin did not see it as an end in itself, but as something to be amended. He incorporated developments in his own thinking resulting from the comments and discoveries of others.

Darwin was elated by the success of his book but it was not long before the critical reviews began. Some were jealous that they had not been able to do what he had done. There was a vicious attack from Richard Owen in *The Edinburgh Review* and another by Sedgwick who accused him of 'deserting the inductive tract … which leads to physical truth'. Even Darwin's cousin, Hensleigh Wedgwood, was concerned about the unanswered question on the origin of life itself. However, Darwin gained 'intense satisfaction' from Hooker's approval and from his and Lyell's 'generous and unselfish sympathy'.

John Murray, the publisher of all Darwin's work

Joseph Hooker, Director of Kew Gardens and close friend and supporter of Darwin

What was it that some scientists objected to in Darwin's ideas? One problem was still that though many of them had accepted the idea of some kind of evolutionary process (see pp. 18 and 19) most held on to the idea that God was the one all-powerful creator of living things. Other more specific problems were:

1. They could accept that perhaps parts of a body could adapt over time, but what started the change in the first place?
2. Why were there such large gaps in the fossil record?
3. How could a complicated structure like the eye be made by natural selection?
4. Darwin's theory depended on a belief that the earth was much older than most of his contemporaries thought.
5. If various characteristics in living things adapted them to survive, how were they passed down to future generations?

The answers Darwin gave to these questions are explanations that many people now take for granted:

1. Changes begin by pure chance, and then, if they prove to be beneficial, they are perpetuated.
2. Geological changes to the earth have removed much of the fossil record.
3. Complicated structures evolve because lots of very tiny changes add up over a very long period of time.
4. The earth proved to be even older than he had calculated!
5. Inheritance is vital for evolution but Darwin did not understand all the processes by which this occurred. The intricacies of genetics were later uncovered by Gregor Mendel.

Nevertheless a small core of scientists passionately believed in and argued for the content of *The Origin*. Apart from his devoted friends Charles Lyell and Joseph Hooker, there was T H Huxley whose brilliant defence of Darwin at the Oxford Debate is described below. Another notable supporter was the

Thomas Henry Huxley who defended Darwin so fiercely that he was known as 'Darwin's bulldog'

WELLCOME INSTITUTE LIBRARY, LONDON

banker and writer John Lubbock, later Lord Avebury, who, as a child, learned much about natural history from his walks in the gardens with Darwin at Down. He later wrote a book on the social behaviour of insects and in 1869 was elected to Parliament where he introduced science to the school curriculum and was responsible for some of the first wildlife conservation laws.

John Lubbock, who learned much from Darwin as a boy and later gave important support to his theory

MARY EVANS PICTURE LIBRARY

41

ABOVE *Charles Darwin showing an ape the likeness between them (Cartoon from the* London Sketch Book, *1874)*

RIGHT *The Bishop of Oxford in a cartoon from* Vanity Fair

FACING PAGE *A cartoon from* Fun *(1872), just after Darwin's book* On the Expression of the Emotions *was published*

RIGHT *Letterpress engraving of cartoon from* Punch's Almanack, *1881*

The Origin excited the interest not only of scientists and thinkers but of the general public. It was unusual for the public to become so involved in scientific debate, but Darwin's theory had fascinating and shocking implications for them – were human beings related to apes? Though Darwin avoided direct discussion of this issue in *The Origin*, he did put mankind on a level with other animals and did conclude by saying that,

'Much light will be thrown on the origin of Man and his history'.

Numerous journals caricatured Darwin as an ape, and FitzRoy wrote that he could not 'find anything "ennobling" in the thought of being a descendant of even the most ancient Ape'.

The Great Oxford Debate

The first major test of how Darwin's theory was to be received by the scientific world was at the meeting of the British Association for the Advancement of Science at Oxford in June 1860. Darwin's book had become the main topic of conversation in scientific circles but Darwin himself remained secluded at Down, preferring fate to take its course and knowing that his supporters would champion his cause.

The Bishop of Oxford, nicknamed 'Soapy Sam' Wilberforce, was invited to reply to a paper on 'civilization according to the Darwinian hypothesis'. Addressing a crowded meeting, the bishop paused during his monologue, turned to Huxley and asked whether it was on his grandfather's or his grandmother's side that he was descended from an ape. Huxley was ready with a reply (no-one remembers the exact words) that he would prefer a miserable ape to a man who employs his great faculties and influence for the purpose of ridicule. He and Hooker between them managed to silence the bishop and with him much of the opposition from the Church. Huxley was soon to earn himself the nickname of 'Darwin's Bulldog'.

Darwin's ideas were fully aired at the debate and today many people accept them as fact. However, there are a substantial number of Creationists who continue to reject Darwin's theories, even in the light of the overwhelming weight of evidence published since.

The impact of Darwin's views was felt in many other parts of the world as well as Britain. A German translation was published in 1860 and by mid-January of 1860 the first reprint had been issued in America. Negotiations followed for translations into Dutch (1861), French (1862), Russian (1864) and Swedish (1869). *The Origin* was translated into ten European languages within Darwin's lifetime. Others came later: the first Japanese edition was published in 1896 and the first Chinese edition in 1903. Like Darwin's *Journal of Researches*, it has remained in print ever since.

MAN·IS·BVT·A·WORM.

THAT TROUBLES OUR MONKEY AGAIN.

Female descendant of Marine Ascidian:—"REALLY, MR. DARWIN, SAY WHAT YOU LIKE ABOUT MAN; BUT I WISH YOU WOULD LEAVE MY EMOTIONS ALONE!"

SUGGESTED ILLUSTRATION
"DR. DARWIN'S MOVEMENTS AND HABITS OF CLIMBING PLANTS."
(See Murray's List of Forthcoming Works.)

Darwin in a cartoon by Linley Sambourne from Punch *(1875)*

DARWIN DID NOT STOP WORKING after the publication of *The Origin*. He carried on writing but also made time for more practical research. There were many topics that he had looked into during his work on *The Origin* and promised himself that he would return to in more detail.

Orchids and climbing plants

One subject that had intrigued Darwin was the shape and habits of plants. In the meadows and hedgerows of his own garden at Down and in his greenhouse, he found the specimens and the inspiration he needed.

Although Darwin never thought of himself as a botanist, his contributions to the subject were as significant as the formulation of his theory of natural selection. Many observations which today are seen as 'text-book' classics were made by Charles Darwin. By studying the various structures of flowers, particularly orchids, Darwin 'found that nearly all parts of the flower are co-adapted for fertilisation by insects. Darwin's book on orchids, *On the Various Contrivances by which Orchids are Fertilised by Insects*, was published in 1862. He later kept most of his orchids in the hothouse in the garden at Down.

Darwin was greatly influenced by the American botanist, Asa Gray, and Gray's paper on the coiling of tendrils of plants stimulated him to undertake his own experiments on the subject. The differences between the two unrelated species of bryony in the hedgerows at Down, led Darwin to explain how each had developed in a different way due to natural selection. His book, *The Movements and Habits of Climbing Plants*, was published in 1865.

Darwin's next task was to publish the vast catalogue of facts and observations on domestication and breeding that were the result of the years of pigeon breeding and earlier plant experiments. The material was summarised by Darwin in two volumes and published as *The Variation of Animals and Plants Under Domestication* in 1868.

'The Descent of Man'

Having taken refuge for several years in the study of plants, Darwin knew that he must finally address himself, in published form, to the logical extension of the ideas presented in *The Origin*.

Darwin had realised from the time he opened his first notebook on transmutation that he 'could not avoid the belief that man must come under the same law'. Accordingly, despite the controversial reaction to *The Origin*, he embarked on the *Descent of Man* (1871) so that 'no honourable man should accuse me of concealing my views'.

It was in this book that Darwin used the term 'evolution' for the first time in its modern

RIGHT *Orchids were very popular in Victorian England. This is an illustration from* The Practical Gardener *(c.1870)*

BELOW *Darwin's book* On the Various Contrivances by which Orchids are Fertilised by Insects *(1862)*

context. He subsequently discussed his transmutation theory in terms of 'evolution' more fully in the sixth and final edition of *The Origin* (1872).

The Descent of Man renewed the impassioned debate started by *The Origin* because it stated openly what *The Origin* had only hinted at: that mankind was directly descended from animals. *The Times* issued a strong warning about the religious and social consequences of the *Descent of Man*:

> *'If our humanity be merely the natural product of the modified faculties of the brutes, most earnest-minded men will be compelled to give up those motives by which they have attempted to live noble and virtuous lives, as founded on a mistake …'*

Secluded at Down, Darwin felt the tremors of the reaction to his work but was relatively unaffected by them. He doggedly carried on with research that would support his theories.

RIGHT *The title page of* The Descent of Man *which shocked people by suggesting that they were descended from apes*

BELOW *An illustration from* The Descent of Man

THE
DESCENT OF MAN,
AND
SELECTION IN RELATION TO SEX.

BY CHARLES DARWIN, M.A., F.R.S., &c.

IN TWO VOLUMES—Vol. II.

WITH ILLUSTRATIONS.

LONDON:
JOHN MURRAY, ALBEMARLE STREET.
1871.

[*The right of Translation is reserved.*]

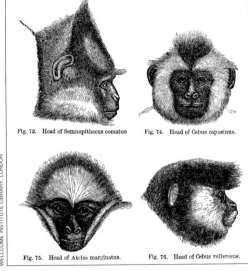

Fig. 73. Head of Semnopithecus comatus

Fig. 74. Head of Cebus capucinus.

Fig. 75. Head of Ateles marginatus.

Fig. 76. Head of Cebus vellerosus.

'The Expression of the Emotions in Man and Animals'

Darwin had been interested in human facial expressions for a very long time. When his children were babies, he carefully observed their faces and behaviour, making notes on crying and smiling in his 'baby book'. He thought that these innate expressions and some behaviour patterns were evidence for links with animals, demonstrating that animals, as well as human beings, express emotions such as joy and guilt. He identified 'fixed action patterns', with reference to observations by his grandfather, Erasmus Darwin, on instinctive behaviour in dogs.

As soon as he had finished work on *The Descent of Man*, Darwin launched into his next book which drew together all his observations on emotion in human beings and animals, *The Expression of the Emotions in Man and Animals*. The book was published in 1872 and pioneered the subject of animal behaviour. It was also unusual in being one of the earliest books in which photographs were published.

ABOVE *Darwin's book,* The Expression of the Emotions in Man and Animals, *was one of the first to use photographs as illustrations*

BELOW *Illustrations from* The Expression of the Emotions

Fig. 18. Chimpanzee disappointed and sulky. Drawn from life by Mr. Wood.

THE MOVEMENT OF PLANTS AND THE ACTION OF WORMS

Bessy Darwin, (c.1865) the only child left at home

DURING THE LAST TEN YEARS OR SO of his life, with his major works published and all the children but Bessy gone away, the only obstacle to Darwin's investigations was his own poor health which made him feel 'old and helpless'. He would still try to circle the Sandwalk every day and spent many hours observing plants and creatures in the garden. The old gardener, Lettington, totally unsympathetic to his master's way of working, when asked about the state of Darwin's health, is said to have replied,

'He moons about in the garden, and I have seen him standing doing nothing before a flower for ten minutes at a time. If he only had something to do, I really believe he would be better'.

Darwin was now able to devote more time to the observation of plants. For many years he experimented with cross-fertilising and self-fertilising plants. He realised that the hybrids resulting from cross-fertilisation were more

Charles Darwin in old age by John Collier

FAR RIGHT *Drawings from Horace Darwin's scrapbook*

vigorous than those that were self-fertilised. *The Effects of Cross and Self Fertilisation in the Vegetable Kingdom*, published in the autumn of 1876, formed a complement to his work on orchids. All the experiments were conducted by Darwin, his staff and his children, in the experimental beds by the greenhouses.

Darwin's son Frank was also fascinated by the movement of plants and had studied plant physiology with Julius Sachs in Germany. After the death of his wife, Frank came to live at Down House with his young son Bernard and was therefore able to spend a considerable amount of time helping his father with the practical work involved in his researches.

According to Frank, 'the central idea ... is that the movements of plants in relation to light, gravitation, &c., are modifications of a spontaneous tendency to revolve'. Between them they showed that 'in accordance with the principles of evolution it was impossible to account for climbing plants having been developed in so many widely different groups, unless all kinds of plants possess some slight power of movement of an analogous kind.' This work was published in 1880 as *The Power of Movement in Plants*.

Insectivorous plants

During July 1860, while visiting Emma's sister in the Ashdown Forest, Darwin had 'amused [himself] with a few observations on the insect-catching power of *Drosera*' (the common sun-dew). He discovered that the plants produced a fluid 'closely analogous to the digestive fluid of an animal'. His experiments were pursued at leisure, and the resulting book, *Insectivorous Plants*, was not published until fifteen years later, in July 1875.

Blue Hepatic   Convolvulus

'The Different Forms of Flowers on Plants of the Same Species'

In 1877 Darwin published a compilation of several papers on 'heterostyled flowers'. He was particularly pleased with his original discovery relating to primroses in that the long-styled primrose is not fully fertile unless set with pollen from a short-styled flower. The fascinating implication of this confirmed the conclusion that Darwin had already reached – that self-fertilisation is not as effective as cross-fertilisation. The primroses were presumably once self-fertilising, but had evolved 'contrivances' by which to cross-fertilise.

Horace Darwin on the Sandwalk

The action of worms

Perhaps Darwin's longest running sequence of observations was gathered into his last book: *The Formation of Vegetable Mould Through the Action of Worms with Observations on their Habits.* Again, much of the study of the worms was achieved with the assistance of Frank.

Long beforehand, Darwin's uncle, Josiah Wedgwood, had suggested to Darwin that the 'apparent sinking of superficial bodies is due, ... to the large quantity of fine earth continually brought up to the surface by worms in the form of castings'.

Darwin first carried out experiments by spreading chalk and cinders over the surface of the ground and noting how far beneath it they sunk over a period of time. Darwin's son Horace had always been fascinated by anything mechanical, and during his engineering apprenticeship, he designed a special instrument for his father to measure the action of the worms. Horace carried out many

detailed experiments and observations with the help of the instrument, and demonstrated the power of the worm to work geological changes and make beneficial modifications to the ground.

As well as measuring the amount of soil worms could displace, Darwin also carried out, with the help of his family, many other experiments to test the behaviour of worms. He kept worms in tubes in his study and observed them at night in the light from a bull's-eye lantern with slides of red and blue glass. The whole family joined in a test to find out what worms could hear. Bernard played the metal whistle, Frank the bassoon, Bessy shouted and Emma played the piano. They were found to be unaffected by all of these, but would react to the vibrations of the piano when placed actually *on* the instrument.

Once again Darwin showed that evolution may be achieved by the cumulative effect of infinitely small changes. His manuscript on worms was published in October 1881, including in the final passage the words,

'Worms have played a more important part in the history of the world than most persons would at first suppose'.

Almost the last act of Darwin's life was to add his amendments to the second edition of this book, printed early in 1882.

Darwin's greenhouse. An engraving from The Century Magazine *(1883)*

ABOVE *A cartoon by Linley Sambourne in* Punch, *1881*

LEFT *The instrument designed by Horace Darwin for measuring the vertical movements of a specially sited stone, and a page from the 'Wormstone notebook' where he recorded the measurements taken from the instrument*

EPILOGUE

One of Charles Darwin's visiting cards

CHARLES DARWIN DIED ON 19 April 1882, and was buried in Westminster Abbey where his scientific status is properly acknowledged.

In the conclusion to his great book, *On the Origin of Species*, Darwin wrote:

'It is interesting to contemplate a tangled bank, clothed with many plants of many kinds, with birds singing on the bushes, with various insects flitting about, and with worms crawling through the damp earth, and to reflect that these elaborately constructed forms, so different from each other, and dependent upon each other in so complex a manner, have all been produced by laws acting around us.'

Darwin almost certainly had part of the Down estate in mind when writing this. Its grounds and environs were Darwin's 'tangled bank' and its birds and insects and the worms crawling through its damp earth, provided him with evidence for what is now considered one of the most important scientific theories ever propounded. This is the attraction of Down House today – that visitors know that *this* was the environment that inspired Darwin, and that it was when circling *this* Sandwalk that many of Darwin's ideas came to him.

Darwin's theory so captures the imagination that it continues to influence popular culture and to stretch scientific thought. From behavioural studies of our closest living relatives in the animal kingdom, to genetic engineering, the principles of evolution are being employed for the benefit of mankind and the environment. Darwin's influence reaches ever widening fields of research as we continue to seek the answer to that still fascinating 'mystery of mysteries': the origin of living things.

The funeral of Charles Darwin at Westminster Abbey in 1882. From The Graphic